ImPerfectly Perfect Mom

DENNA MICHELLE TRIGGS

Copyright © 2016 Denna Michelle Triggs

All rights reserved.

ISBN-13: 978-0692628386 (Be Inspired, LLC)

ISBN-10: 069262838X

DEDICATION

To my heavenly father, God,

To my mother Sylvia Reed

To my father Leon Williams,

To my husband Jeron Triggs

To the awesome children I have had the privilege to parent

CJ, Christian, Christianna, Jaxson, Taylor, & Sierra,

To my spiritual parents Pastor & Lady Burns,

To my siblings, family, friends, and church family you all have help to shape and form me into the woman I am today by teaching me where my true treasures lie. I love each and every one of you.

CONTENTS

Acknowledgments		Page i
Introduction		Page 3
Chapter 1	Respect	Page 5
Chapter 2	Finances	Page 15
Chapter 3	Distractions	Page 31
Chapter 4	Co-Parenting	Page 39
Chapter 5	Child Discipline	Page 49
Chapter 6	Responsible	Page 55
Chapter 7	Preserve	Page 61
Closing		Page 69
Resources		Page 70
About the Author		Page 71
Suggested Readings		Page 72

ACKNOWLEDGMENTS

I am deeply thankful to the mothers, children and families who have allotted me the pleasure to touch, shape and help them to be inspired, and achieve their goals.

I also want to thank all the mothers whose stories are woven into my story as a mom; who appear in this book. I have entered them into my tips through the books.

Thanks to all the authors I know who helped me to know it is possible for me to publish a book: Dr. Anthony D. Burns, Robin L. Burns, Min. Nina Haliburton, Sharon Brumfield, Sharan Fifer, and Dr. Melissa Bonds.

To Kenya Hayes: You are that little sent angel helping me to organize my thinking for this book. Thanks for being my editor and having faith in my ability to produce this book.

To Jeron Triggs, Delta Reed, Monique Davis, Latoya Denton and Lakeeta Watts: Thanks for guidance, questions, and suggestions on how to make my book better.

INTRODUCTION

DEAR IMPERFECTLY PERFECT MOM,

Did you know there is no such thing as a perfect mom?

You may be shocked, because mothers are always being told how to raise their children, by government agencies, TV shows, toy companies, and other mothers who pretend to be experts at raising children. It's no surprise that many moms, especially first-time mothers, are worried about doing everything wrong. A mom imagines being the perfect parent to her perfect children. But things never seem to happen that way. Many moms think that they have failed. They are hard on themselves and feel guilty. Mothers need to realize that they have a job no man could possibly accomplish. Moms are making their families and their behaviors fit into the world standards of family. Standards mothers piece together, and think are right. Standards held by moms is a reflection of all the advice they have received from government agencies, television, toy companies, their mothers, and other mothers who pretend to be experts on raising children. Trying to fit into the world's standards is like trying to fit into someone else's skin! Even if you wanted to (and you can't), you would only succeed in making yourself and your children, unhappy.

So what is a mom to do? The beautiful reality is that each mom has her own distinct and perfectly useable way of being a mom. Some mothers like to play with their children, others like more time to themselves. Some moms spend their days working at home, some work outside the home. Some enjoy cooking and fussing, reading stories and nursery rhymes, playing football and basketball with their children; others honestly choose to be around adults. Some moms talk and want help with the ups and downs, while others go it alone. Each must discover the way that is best for her, and that way will look like no other's.

Finding your own way is a matter of being honest with yourself. Knowing your likes and dislikes, skills and abilities, triggers or panic buttons, sensitivities, and circumstances. Then build on your strengths, and accept and develop those you are not strong in. This means: Don't fight yourself! For example, if you really hate math and your seven-year-old needs help, don't do it. Instead, try finding a tutor that can help with it. Then ask the child to show you what he or she has learned. This way the child will still get the joy of having you involved in their math work. Understand that you will make some mistakes. All moms do. This understanding attitude will reward you in two ways. The first way, you will be happier, and less likely to burnout or give up. The second way is your child will reap the same benefits! Children often copy the attitudes and personality traits of their parents. For example, if you are tense and a perfectionist, you may be telling your child to be challenging, and a doubter. On the other hand, if you are relaxed and accepting with yourself and others, chances are your child will be, too.

If you have been feeling depressed, defeated, discouraged, or disappointed by the life of being a mom, Imperfectly Perfect Mom is for you. This book is a collection of letters to mothers just like you. Accompanied with the letters are tips and pointers to assist you with becoming a more confident mom.

Use this book to develop your knowledge, habits and confidence you need to be a successful mom! Remember it is ok to be imperfect and that is what makes you perfect.

RESPECT

DEAR DISRESPECTED MOM,

Have you ever had your child roll their eyes, stomp their feet and tell you, "I am not doing nothing", and meant it! Well I have.

Here is my story'

I got married and immediately started my family. I had an awesome bonus daughter from my first husband, who was 3 at the time. For those who don't know my bonus daughter was my step daughter. I do not like that word step it makes me think of Snow White's evil step mother and I am far from evil. I love bonus which is in addition to. I got pregnant soon after getting married. In the beginning everything was peaches and cream. I was her Denna. But when her dad and her mom stepped in, it went downhill. I could not raise her the way I wanted to. When I raised her how I wanted we got along. I treated her how I wanted to be treated. "A person is a person no matter how small." My favorite quote by Dr. Seuss. When she would talk I listened. When she did good I praised her, when she was naughty, I showed her the right way. Unfortunately I was alone in this process. Her parents got upset. I had to include her mother and father. I hear you saying, "What does her momma have to do it?" She has a lot to do with it. I cannot raise her child how I would like to. I'm here to assist my

> A PERSON'S A PERSON
> NO MATTER HOW SMALL.
>
> Dr. Seuss

bonus daughter's parents. I had to deal with raising a child in ways I didn't agree with.

My first husband wanted to raise his daughter by the "ROD." He strongly believe spare the rod spoil the child. His philosophy is, "if you put fear in them when they are young, you won't have problems later". I believe in modeling the desired behaviors, and they will get it. I say save the rod for when it is needed. I never want any of my kids bonus, biological or God, to fear me. I want them to respect me. Once they get old enough and think they are bigger than me they will no longer fear me. When they do not fear me is the moment we're fighting. According to the Merriam-Webster Dictionary fear is, "an unpleasant often strong emotion caused by anticipation or awareness of danger". So if you're instilling fear in your children they will only react when they feel they are in danger. So when you go to hit them they anticipate danger and either withdraw themselves or fight back.

Merriam-Webster says, "respect is a feeling of admiring someone or something that is good, valuable, important etc..." Another definition is, to act in a way which shows that you are aware of someone's rights wishes etc. That means kids will behave simply because they know you want them to. No threatening them, no beating them, just simple clear-cut asking and them doing. I believe me treating my daughter with respect helped her learn respect. "Monkey see, Monkey do!"

Okay Smart Aleck! You think just because you gave birth to your child that means that he or she have to automatically respect you, you're dead WRONG! There's that other saying "Respect is earned not given."

Respectfully yours,

Denna Michelle, A Respectful mother

PS: SHOW RESPECT EVEN TO PEOPLE WHO DON'T DESERVE IT; NOT AS A REFLECTION OF THEIR CHARACTER AS A REFLECTION OF YOUR. –DAVE WILLIS

How to Earn Respect from Your Child

Respect is earned by giving respect. What you give will come back. The Boomerang effect. Giving respect means considering their thoughts and feelings. Respect is a verb or an action word. Meaning you need to do something. Something you should do is listen to your kids, give them self-worth, and build self-esteem.

RULE # 1 ACTIVELY LISTEN TO THEM! Eye contact and the ability to repeat what your child says is active listening.

RULE # 2 SELF-WORTH The way you treat your child is sign of the respect you have for yourself. "Children should be treated as children"

RULE #3 SELF-ESTEEM Everyone has dignity and worth. Your child is valuable and unique. Let them know. Praise them!

RULE # 1 ACTIVE LISTENING

Let's talk about listening. Listening is an important skill that everyone seems not to have. I am not just talking about using your ears to hear what your children are saying, but actively listening. The majority of children believe their parents are too distracted to even listen to them. Are you too busy on your electronic devices? Your phone, laptop, computer, IPad or tablet or maybe watching TV.

62 percent of kids say their parents are distracted when they are trying to talk to them. According to Highlights magazine's 2014 State of the Kid survey

results, an annual survey that gives children ages 6 to12 a national platform to share their views and feelings about major topics. Highlights surveyed 1,521 children – including both Highlights readers and non-readers on parental distractions. When asked what distracts their parents, cell phones (28 percent) were the top response, followed by (25 percent), work (16 percent), and TV (13 percent). In total, technology – phones, TV and laptops – accounted for 51 percent of the responses. Let's do better for our kids; they have a lot of important things to say.

Highlights also stated "When it comes to finding focused time to talk to parents, kids say the best time is during a meal (33 percent), closely followed by bedtime (29 percent) and in the car (18 percent). They know their parents are really listening when parents look at them (56 percent), respond (28 percent) and stop doing everything else (11 percent)". Going back to rule of active listening.

Active listening is just that A .C.T.I.V.E.

Attention
Comment
Table
Indicate
Value
Effective

Attention make sure you are paying attention when your child is talking. Not on Facebook, Instagram, Twitter, the computer or phone, but giving them your undivided attention. Look them in the eyes another sign of respect. "Monkey See Monkey Do." If they see you doing it they will do it.

Comment is just simply saying something when there is a pause. Rephrase what you heard, make sure you are hearing your child correctly. An example would be you saying, "Sounds like you are trying to say this...." or "What I am hearing is..." or "If I'm correct you're saying...." or "Did you mean...." Add what your child is saying at the end.

Table is the hardest one for most people including myself. Table your judgment. Let your child talk! Wait to give them your opinion. Interrupting is a waste of time and makes the child more upset. Interrupting will cause them to disengage or stop listening to you. Even lash out because of anger. Then they will never hear what you were trying to say. They need to hear what you want them to stop doing or more importantly, what you want them to start doing. Allow your child to finish their point before you speak and don't interrupt with blowups or even negative comments that can also cause them to get angry.

Indicate why you are waiting to respond to your child. You have to show them that you are listening. Show them that you are listening to them with your body. Look in their eyes, show facial expression, such as smiling, surprise, and serious looks. Nodding in agreement and making sure your body posture is inviting. These are indicators of active listening. Encouraging your child to express him or herself, and then they will ultimately let you express yourself. Which is a sign of value.

KEY POINT: If you want your child to listen to you, you must listen to them not just hear them.

Value what you are hearing from your child. According to the book <u>A Primer on Communication Studies,</u> we forget about half of what we hear immediately after hearing it, recall 35 percent after eight hours, and recall 20 percent after a day. Listening understanding, and valuing what we listen to is something we all can learn to do. You value what your children are saying. By getting information, understanding the information, and learning from that information. After all of that it is time to respond.

 Your response needs to be effective. Your response should be one that shows you value what your child has to say; and will not attack them or put them down. However, you will respond openly and honestly, you will need let the child know that you want them to listen to you in a calm and clear manner. In turn he or she will respond to you in a calm and clear way. Again, monkey see monkey do.

RULE # 2 SELF WORTH

The way you treat your child signifies the amount of respect you have for yourself. "Children should be treated as children." They are children not small adults. Children lack knowledge, wisdom, and experience and for that reason they are immature and should be allowed to be. Some of us seem to expect our child to act like an adult. But they are still learning and it is our job to teach.

RULE # 3 SELF ESTEEM

Everyone has dignity and worth. Your child is valuable and unique. Let them know. Praise them!

Now, let's talk about praising them. Praises give you motivation it also gives children motivation to keep on doing what you want them to do, or stop doing what you do not want them to do. Someone may ask, how do I motivate my child through praise? There are two types of children to praise. The first is the "Obedient" child. The second one is the still working on being obedient. Let's say your child loves to do what you say, that will be your "Obedient" child. The other child has to be told to do something 50 times. This is the still working on being obedient child. You're probably thinking why should I praise the child that is taking responsibility to be obedient, accepting the direction that you give them, and just wants to always do what's right? The answer is simple! So they continue to do the things you want them to do; so that they strive for more. Here's how you praise him.

> Tell him how great of a job he is doing, on his set tasks. (Be as specific as possible)
>
> Share opportunities to grow and do better. This way he will never feel like what he is doing is being overlooked, but appreciated. This helps him to keep getting better.

Now, the who is still working on being obedient, is the child that avoids responsibility. That child that needs to be told every step more than once. That child that needs to be supervised. That child that must be bribed into doing whatever you ask them to do. It is very important for them to be praised. Praising them will help them to do what you say the first time given without supervision or a bribe. This will not happen overnight it is a process. Try using positive reinforcement instead of bribes. Positive reinforcement is praising them for a behavior with the goal of getting a better chance of that behavior being repeated in the future. Here's how you praise him.

Tell him how great of a job he is doing, on his set tasks. (Be as specific as possible)

Share opportunities to grow and do better. This way he will never feel like what he is doing is being overlooked, but appreciated.

This helps him to keep getting better. Did you go back and read the "Obedient" child praise list. Yes, they are the same. Some parents say this is hard work and doesn't work. Create a system! Positive reinforcement can turn into more work for a parent to inforce and track (tracking to see whether it is working) without some sort of system for structure and tracking. There are various templates, charts and tables out there for parents to use. Make sure it works for you and your child.

You must simply believe that they work. Believe in yourself and your child. What's worse having your child fear you and lose them or respecting your child and keeping them?

FINANCES

DEAR FINANCIALLY CHALLENGED MOM,

The struggle is real. The days of barely making it, living pay check to pay check and being "Tax Rich". That's my phrase for when you get your tax refund and buy unnecessary items or stuff you would not normally buy any other time of the year.

I have never really been "Tax Rich"; because I was a teacher who barely made any money in the first place, and needed my refund to live off of in the summer. I had to apply for food stamps just to make sure me and my three kids at that time had enough to eat during the summer. We needed 3 meals and 2 snack we was at home all day no school or work I was responsible for all the meals. I remember having to make deals with the landlord to do administrative work or cleaning just to offset some of my rent.

My money was truly funny.

During the next school year my church had a small group that used a financial curriculum because I wanted to be in control of my finances I invested in the curriculum. The curriculum discussed financial planning; which included budgeting, paying off debt and most importantly PAYING YOURSELF FIRST, which is fancy for SAVING. I began by quickly saving an emergency fund and living on a budget. I knew in the summer this would be very important.

After sticking to my budget for a couple of months, I realize I still would not have enough to maintain my same lifestyle in the summer even with my tax refund. So I had to remember what the financial curriculum said about multiple streams of income. So I opened up to 2 more streams of income. When summer rolled around, I had enough money saved to be able to maintain my school year lifestyle. I was able to go on a vacation and pay off debt with my tax refund. It felt awesome to call the car finance office and ask, what is my pay-off amount and pay it. One of the best day of my life. I then was able to just give the car away and get me another one because my financial plan was working.

GET YOUR FINANCES UNDER CONTROL!!

Sincerely,

Denna M. Triggs, Financial Planner

PS: HOW YOU LIVE TOMORROW IS BUILT ON HOW YOU PLAN TODAY! ~ DENNA M. TRIGGS

FINANCIALLY PLANNING FOR YOUR FUTURE

Money, Money, Money! Can you really live without it? Nope! Everyone needs money to live in our day and age. We all get it from different places. Moms get it from working, having businesses or even the government. It does not matter where you get your money from you can still get a handle on your money. Many moms feel that they do not make enough money or have a good handle over their money to meet their family needs or even buy things they want.

This section will give you steps to follow to take control over your money and make it go further.

      Step 1 Create a Financial Plan

      Step 2 Create a monthly budget to follow

      Step 3 Saving

      Step 4 Use a Financial Institute

STEP 1 CREATE A FINANCIAL PLAN

The first step in taking control of your money is a Financial Planning. A financial plan is setting goals. Setting financial goals means figuring out where to be financially and priorities your needs and wants. Your financial goals can be short (less than 6months) or long term (greater than 6 months), small or large, but needs to be SMART.

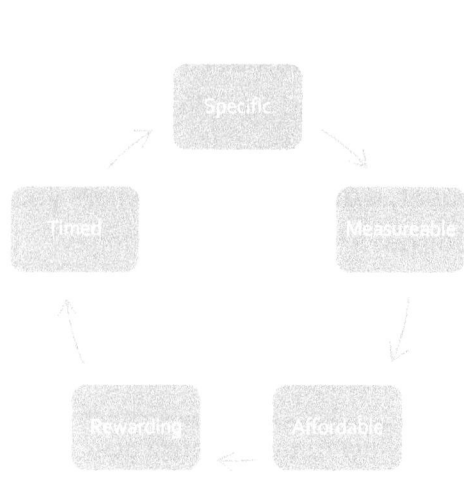

Specific: clearly defined. Exactly what you want to happen with your money

Measurable: able to be measured. Amount to spend or save

Affordable: reasonable price. Within your income & budget

Rewarding: Providing Satisfaction. Minimal meets needs

Timed: Made to occur in a set time. Realistic time frame

Some examples of financial goals could be:

1. Saving $20,000 for college funds in 10 years by adding $100 each month in an interest drawing account.
2. Buying a $5,000 car within a year
3. Paying off credit card debt of $355 in 6 month at $60 per month
4. Saving for Christmas gifts $200 each month for a year totaling $2,400
5. Saving for family vacation to Disney world flights cost 1,000 hotel cost $550 food & entertainment $1,200 Total $2,750 Save $230 each month for a year.

Now that you have some examples, let us write down some SMART financial goals you would want to achieve and keep them in mind as you read this section.

Needs vs Wants

Now that you have a few SMART financial goals in minds you must identify if your goal is a need or a want. Knowing the difference between everyday needs and wants makes a big difference in the success of your financial plan and how likely you are able to reach your goal.

Needs are things you have to have. Needs are basic necessities such as food, clothing, shelter, transportation, and medical needs. Needs should always come first. Everything that goes beyond this such as lavish food, a big house, name brand clothes or a new car is a want. That does not mean you only have to buy the necessities. Life is meant to be enjoyed not merely existing. Treat yourself and your family to some wants, but do so when you can afford it. Wants bring joy to the family only when they are a part of the family financial plan.

BUDGET GUIDELINES

1. Use cash not credit card for buying things
2. Look for bargains
3. Signup for coupons and free items
4. Stay in your budget
5. Write down what you spend money on. (actual)
6. Save your receipts
7. Keep a positive attitude about budgeting
8. Reward yourself when you create your budget and again after you stick to it.

STEP 2 CREATE A MONTHLY BUDGET TO FOLLOW

After you created a financial plan you break it down into a monthly, quarterly and yearly budget. What is a budget? A budget is monthly, quarterly and/or yearly saving and spending plan for your financial goals.

It is your guide for achieving your goals within a certain time frame. A budget allows you plan and track your money rather than careless spending. Your budget should help you achieve your goals. It should be flexible, realistic and balanced. Your budget should always equal $0.00 (zero). Every dollar needs to be accounted for. If there is any money left over you can add it to the savings or entertainment category. The first step in budgeting is figuring out where your money come from, which is your income. This could be work, child support, government assistance (cash benefits, food stamps, WIC, etc.) anything that helps with meeting those basic needs. The next step is figuring out where the money goes, which is your expenses. There are two kinds of expenses: Fixed and Flexible. Fixed expenses are those expenses that are the same each time. Fixed expenses could be rent, car payments, loan payments, etc. Flexible expenses are those expenses that change each time. Some flexible expenses could be food, gas for car, heating, electricity, etc.

A good approach to figure out your budget is to make a monthly budget worksheet. This worksheet should include all of your income and expenses (fixed and Flexible) the expected, actual and the difference (There are samples at the end of the section). Keeping track of expected is just what you believe the total amount for the period will be. The actual is after the time period you added up exactly what you spent. Keeping track of actual amounts tells you where your money is going. The difference is just you subtracting the expected from the actual. Keeping track of difference tells you how to adjust your budget or how much more money you need to make.

STEP 3 SAVINGS

A fixed expense item on your budget should be savings. Saving money unlocks so many doors for you and helps you achieve your financial goals. With this as a part of your budget it becomes your monthly savings plan. Once you make your savings plan you can begin saving money each month to get you to your financial goal. Your savings plan should include these steps:

1. Know the amount you need to save
2. Know how much you can save each month
3. Pay yourself first
4. Make a "Savings Schedule" (example in the back of this section)

STEP 4 USE A FINANCIAL INSTITUTE

A financial institute is a place that focuses on dealing with money transactions, such as investments, loans and deposits. Traditional financial institutes include banks, trust companies, insurance companies and investment dealers. There are also non-traditional financial institutes which include, credit unions, pre-paid debit cards, title loan and check cashing stores. There are many more out there, these are just a few.

Using a financial institute is another step in controlling your finances. One may wonder, "Why is important to use a financial institute? While they may help you create a financial plan, they also have small interest growing savings accounts and help you achieve your financial goals. Financial institutes allow you to transfer money from one place to another. You can do through check writing, telephone wires, ATM (automated teller machine) and online.

Financial institutes provides you with the ability to gain interest. Thus allowing you to save more money while you achieve your goal. You also receive a regular statement to provide you with the actual break down of how you spent your money. They also provide you with an easy, safe, fast and reliable way to get your paycheck direct deposited into your account. Also but less recommended, financial institutes provide you with credit. Credit or a loan may help you pay for cars, houses, furniture, education and many other things. Be careful with credit make sure you can afford the terms.

Opening an account

To open either a checking or savings account you would need to bring some items with you.

1. Photo Id with signature
2. A secondary id with signature
3. Social security number or Tax id for business
4. Proof of address
5. A completed application and signature card (they will provide or may be found online at most institutes).
6. Cash or check to deposit (amount varies at different institutes)

Checking Account

Having a checking account allows you access to writing checks to pay bills, take money out the ATM, direct deposit, statements, telephone and online banking, and most important the interest to earn money for saving towards your financial goals.

To the moms who never wrote a check before here are some basics.

1. Make sure you put the date where it says date or the person can cash whenever they want. Checks may have expiration date please look for the expiration date most times it is 90 days after the date the check was written/printed.
2. Make sure you write the name of person or business. If you fail to do this anyone can put their name on it and cash the check, and you will still owe who you originally attempted to pay.
3. Most importantly the amount in numbers and in words. You don't want someone to ever put their own amount because they may take more money out of your account then you authorized.
4. Memo section add what payment is for or account number. This let payee know what the money goes toward.
5. Another very important part of the check writing process is your signature. They need your authorization to process the check.

How to Use Your Checking Account

You go to the bank with proper identification needed to open the account you will also need a deposit to put into the account. When you receive your checkbook it will come with a register, the register is used to keep track of your financial transactions with your account. This will also help with your budget and financial plan. You should record in your register when you deposit money, write a check, use the ATM (deposit or withdraw) and taking money out of your account inside the institution.

Savings Account

Savings accounts are those accounts I was talking about that pay interest. They are great to keep your money safe and out of your hands to help you achieve your financial goal.

7 Benefits of a saving account:

1. Earn interest on the money in your account
2. Safe place to save money
3. All or partial amount of paycheck direct deposited
4. Transfer money to & from checking account
5. Withdrawal of money from ATM
6. Online and telephone banking
7. Keep track of your money

ATM Automated Teller Machine

ATMs gives you a stress-free way to do banking like withdrawals, deposits, transfers, payments and balances. An ATM or debit card gives you access to these ways of banking. You will need a personal identification number (PIN) to go along with your card to gain access to your account via ATM. For a small fee your account can be access from an ATM anywhere. An ATM card can j be used at ATMs and debit cards can be used at grocery, department and other stores. They also require you to enter in your PIN. Debit cards when used at stores can also give you access to cash back when you make a purchase. These transaction will show up or post to your account immediately.

Some debit cards give you the option to use your debit card as a credit card. Using your debit card this way you don't have to use your PIN but purchases over a certain amount will require your signature. Also this transaction will not post immediately to your account. They may show as a pending transaction or not show for a couple of days. Check with your financial institution.

ATM TIPS

- Use ATM that are indoor or with good lighting
- Go in groups or at a busy time where you are never alone.
- Sign your card or put check id
- Memorize your PIN never share it and pick number people will not guess.
- Do not let anyone see your PIN when you enter it.
- Put your money away safely before leaving the ATM area so no one knows how much you have.

PREPAID CARD

More and more people are using prepaid cards. One reason is you can't or won't open a checking account. Maybe you don't want to use a bank, or banks will not let you open an account based on your credit or check writing history. Another reason is you cannot go into debt. If the money is not on your card, you can't spend it.

When it comes to spending prepaid cards work very similar to debit cards. Anywhere you can use a credit card you can use your prepaid card. Remembering you must add your own funds. You can add funds to your card when you purchase the card. You can re-load using some of the following ways:

•Set up direct deposit to the card

•Bring cash to a retail store that can add funds to your card

- Deposit a check with an app that is linked to your card

- Transfer money from your bank account to your prepaid card

A downside to prepaid cards are fees, fees and more fees. Even though things are improving, prepaid cards are known for having high fees and charges for certain purchases. Before the only time it made sense to use a prepaid account was if you could not open an account at a bank or credit union. Keep in mind some cards do offer little to no fees.

Another downside is you're not able to save. Prepaid cards make it very convenient to spend money, but it's hard to save unless you have a savings account thru a bank. Even if you left the money stay on the card there may be fees and you're not accumulating any interest.

When choosing your financial institute to handle your money make sure you do your research and pick the one best for you and your family.

SAMPLE FINANCIAL PLAN:

Sample Financial Plan Worksheet

Monthly Household Net Income: $2,200
Monthly Non-discretionary Expenses: $1,700
Amount Remaining to Save for Goals: $500
Number of Dependents: 0
Your Age: 22
Expected Graduation Date: Just graduated

	Goal # 1	Goal # 2	Goal # 3	Goal # 4
Write Goals Here →	Car down payment	3-month emergency fund	Pay off student loans in 5 years	Start a retirement account
Total cost of each goal	$1,750	$4,500	$2,500	$100,000
Current funds available	$0	$150	$100	$700
Time needed to achieve each goal	2 months	29 months	5 years	30 years
Monthly contribution to achieve goal	$0	$150	$43	$200 from paycheck $80 employer match
Funding source for monthly contribution	Tax refund	Pay check	Pay check	Paycheck & employer match
Method for saving/investing for goal	Checking account	Savings account	Paying on loan	Work retirement account/Mutual funds
Expected interest rate/rate of return	0%	2%	Paying 8.25% interest	9%
Risks	No risks	Disability, expensive emergency	Job loss	Job loss, health, disability
Life	☐	☐	☐	☐
Health (Paid by work)	☐	☐	☐	☒
Disability ($35)	☐	☐	☐	☒
Automobile ($150)	☐	☒	☐	☐
Home/Renters ($20)	☐	☒	☐	☐
Other			Deferment	

Image from MadExpo.us for assistant with creating a financial plan please contact Be Inspired at info@nowbeinspired.com or visit www.nowbeinspired.com

SAMPLE BUDGET:

My Budget
Goal: To save $9600 within one year

Expense	Actual - Last Month	Budget – This Month	Actual – This Month	Over / (Under)
Must Expenses	3178			
Must Fixed	2400			
Mortgage	2000			
Insurance	50			
Student Loan Payment	350			
Must Variable	778			
Electricity	83			
Gas	50			
Water	35			
Food - Groceries	450			
Transportation	150			
Child School Expenses (avg.)	10			
Optional Expenses	245			
Optional Fixed	105			
Cable	60			
Internet	45			
Optional Variable	140			
Books	20			
Movie Rental	20			
Food - Restaurant Meals	100			
Income	4000			
Total Expenses	3423			
Savings	577			

Image from www.budgetingincome.com

for assistant with creating a budget please contact Be Inspired at

info@nowbeinspired.com

or visit

www.nowbeinspired.com

SAMPLE CHECK:

[Check image with numbered annotations: John Doe, 123 Main St, Anywhere US 10111 (1); Date (6); 9011 (11); PAY TO THE ORDER OF (2); dollar box (3); DOLLARS line (4); Your Bank, 456 Main St, Anywhere US 10111 (8); MEMO (5); signature line (7); routing number 123456789 (9); account number 100100239 (10); check number 0090 (11)]

1. **Personal information** about you, the account holder
2. **Recipient line**. Who the check is payable to
3. **The dollar box**. The amount of the check in numerical format
4. **The amount of your check** written out using words instead of numbers
5. **Memo line** for a note (account # or what check is for)
6. **Date line**
7. **Signature line**
8. **Your bank's contact information**
9. **Your bank's ABA routing number**
10. **Your account number** at your bank
11. **Check number** (note that this appears in two places)

SAMPLE DEBIT CARD:

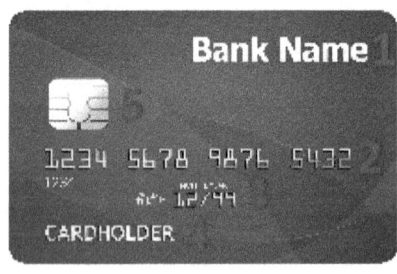

1. **Bank Name** The name of where you bank
2. **Debit Card Number** 16 digtal number that connects card to account
3. **Expiration Date** When your card will expire. (Bank may send another before it expires)
4. **Cardholder** The name of the account holder

5. **Chip** A chip adds another layer of security to cards when used at a chip card reader. During the chip transaction, the chip produces a single-use code to validate the transaction — further protecting cards from unauthorized use.

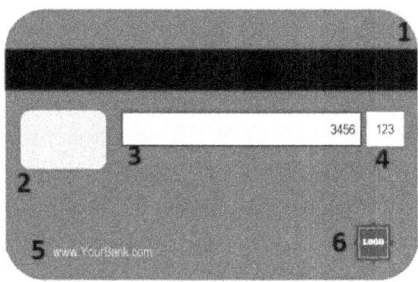

1. **Magnetic strip** What is swiped to get information/make a purchase
2. **Hologram**
3. **Signature** Sign your name
4. **Security Code** 3 or 4 digit number give for added security
5. **Bank Info** Bank contact info
6. **Network Logo** Company who the bank receives service through

Distracted

DEAR DISTRACTED MOM,

When deciding what I was going to write about. My first thought was to write about parenting because I am an AWESOME mom. If I don't toot my own horn who will? Then I thought about writing a children's book, because I own a daycare and all the little children love me. Then my son developed PTSD from the violence and all the funerals we had to attend so he and I decided that he should go and stay with his dad for a while. This led me to write about co-parenting with all the "wonderful" new experiences I was having because he always lived with me.

How I Got Distracted

I began to write out my word web, the outline, and the introduction, I was on a roll. I then started to write about one of my focus area when I got DISTRACTED. I stopped and paused. I went to my advisors, they all were saying I am doing too many things and need to FOCUS on 1 to 3 of them. I could not choose. So one of my advisor suggested a book. I started to read the book. I asked everyone what they think I am good at and what do they depend on me for. I got various responses; but they all went with every single thing that I was doing. That did not help me with narrowing down my FOCUS.

So I figured hey everything that I am doing I was a part of leadership. So I thought about writing a book about leadership. Then one Saturday morning when I was a leadership meeting at my church, they were talking about distraction. We had to pray about one thing we wanted to hear from God about. I of course wanted to focus on what I should write about. I had to focus and pray all while tuning out all the distractions that was going on. I realize at that moment that I was too distracted to hear from God, so I decided to write this section about being distracted.

Some of the distractions that was going on for me was my own cell phone just vibrated in my hands. So I set it down. I also have one of those smart watches and then that vibrated, so I had to take that off my wrist. Once that was off it felt like everybody in the place cell phone was ringing. Then everybody's phone started vibrating. Then after I finally tuned out the rings and vibration of people cell phones more distractions came. Oh my God! I hear people's stomach growling. I heard people walking in and out the sanctuary. I heard people blowing their nose. I heard people clearing their throats. I was so distracted that I could not focus in on what I had to pray for.

How I Got Focused

I then realized that I needed to focus in on what I really wanted. So then I started to tune out everything. I just kept repeating to myself I'm ready, I'm ready, I'm ready! That is how I continued to stay focused. This was confirmation that I needed to write a section in my book about being distracted and staying focused. Distractions can come from anywhere. Distraction can come from your kids, cell phone, or just wanting to play your games.

A distraction free life might not be happen; however, a less distracted life or a distraction free period of time is very possible. In this section I am going to show you six distractions and how to turn those into FOCUS. Now is time to learn how to stay focused!

Focusing,

Denna Michelle, A Focusing Mom

PS: "To do two things at once is to do neither." ~PUBLILIUS SYRUS

6 Mom Distractions

DISTRACTION #1 YOUR PHONE

Do you feel you have to answer every call, reply to every text? Is it realistic to live without a phone? Our phones have become one of the greatest distractions in our lives. Would you say most of us check our phone about 150 times per day? So what do we do?

FOCUS: To limit the distraction of your phone schedule period of time to deal with nonessential calls and texts. It is ok to let your voice mail pick up those calls and you call them back during your scheduled time. If that does not work, turn your phone off for a small period of time and focus on your task. A 10 minute period of complete focus will help you complete the task faster than 2 hours of you being distracted and trying to complete that same task.

DISTRACTION #2 SOCIAL MEDIA

Here a few examples of social media' Facebook, Instagram, and Twitter, just to name a few. I hear you saying "But I use it for my business." Let's just be honest, we don't just go on there to conduct business. We inbox our friend, like this post, add this friend, check this friend's status and then we invite them to our event. And then there is that continual update of notifications.

FOCUS: Here's how you focus when dealing with social media. Choose to turn off the notifications. As a result, you will be able to check your apps on your schedule throughout the day. Separate your business from your personal. Schedule time for business and then schedule for personal so you are not tempted to do personal when you should be doing business. Then set a timer to stop. This is important because social media is designed to consume your time. SET YOUR TIMER!

DISTRACTION #3 TV

So many of us feel like we will miss out if we don't watch the news, Days of Our Lives, Scandal, Empire, etc. I heard someone say the average American watches 4 to 6 hours of TV each day. Most people are only awake for 16 hours that is about a quarter of your day.

FOCUS: This is the most simplistic solution cancel cable or simply never turn the TV on. If this step seems too drastic of a stretch for your family, you'll never regret the simple decision to cancel cable. Your calendar will thank you for the extra time available. Your wallet will thank you for the extra dollars. And you'll quickly wonder why you didn't do it sooner.

DISTRACTION #4 UNORGANIZED

Have you ever walked around your house trying to find diapers, wipes, bottles, toys etc. and have no idea where anything is? My top 2 things I could never find are my keys and my phone. They are normally in places where they should not be like inside the refrigerator or still left in the door or car. Adding the time to not knowing where everything is or goes takes the focus off your child. They continue to be hungry, sleepy and just as frustrated as you.

FOCUS: ORGANIZING PHYSICAL CLUTTER. Discarding unnecessary clutter is a significant form of visual distraction. And the more you have things organized, the less stressed and distracted you are; and you have more time for your kids. Organize your kitchen, your rooms, your counters, and remove unneeded items from your home. You will be surprised at your newfound ability to focus on your kids, yourself and other goals you have.

FOCUS: ORGANIZING YOUR TIME. We all have times of the day in which we get focused a little easier. Schedule your most important work for these times to give yourself the best use of your time. I've started scheduling out my tasks which helps me to stay focused, if it's getting my daughter from soccer practice or remembering to eat lunch before the clock strikes 3pm. Schedule everything and find a system that works. Systems like Google calendar, a planner, a to-do list where you can view, the Disc bound system, AND USE IT! There are other ways to organize your time is just a few.

DISTRACTION #5 MULTI-TASKING

We are constantly distracted by to many tasks having to check texts or email, on the phone while doing housework, paying bills, planning this event, attending this meeting. We don't multitask as well as we think we do. So, when it's time to focus, try to knock out any other distractions.

FOCUS: If you know your child will be hungry feed them, if you know they will be sleepy put them to sleep then try to complete your task. The more you do before you start, the more time you will have to completely focus on the one task, versus having to split your time between your child and your task. Neither gets your full attention and you do not enjoy either. Dinesh Kumar Biran said "We are the generation capable of doing many things at once, without enjoying any of them."

Fortunately, many of these tasks can be completed in less time than we think or even be delegated to someone else. To live with less distraction, if a task can be completed in less than 2 minutes, COMPLETE it in 1-2 minute immediately. If it can be completed by someone else, you delegated it, LET THEM DO IT.

DISTRACTION #6 YOURSELF

Often you may become bored with your motherly tasks and decide to check your phone for a few minutes; or you have several activities to do and your mind keeps jumping from one to the other. So you decide to none of them or my favorite one you decide to go to sleep. Sleep is ok when you have a newborn and they are sleeping, other than that you are allowing yourself to be a distraction.

FOCUS: Accept and find your "mom rhythms". Learn the "mom rhythms" of your day to make the most of them. For example, I do my best work right before bed, so I plan my next day accordingly. Afternoons work well for busy-work, so I get all my task done at this time. Dinnertimes are set aside for my family. Once I have all my task completed I leave most late evenings for entertainment, rest, and guilt-free distraction. Once you find, accepting and understanding your "mom rhythms" you can plan your day and even your week which provides motivation to eliminate distractions during our most useful parts of the day knowing there is chance later to enjoy the guilt-free distractions.

CO-PARENTING

DEAR CO-PARENTING MOM,

When writing this section I was learning to co-parent myself. I recently let my 2 older boys live with their father after about 8 years of me taking care of them by myself with little assistance. This was a decision that was made not because I was frustrated with being a mom. Not because their dad had done anything to change his way of living. This decision was made because my 9 year old was suffering from PTSD.

The "NEWS" today has turned into something that is not a good view on our youth. They show police killing teenagers, teenagers killing teenagers, babies dying in fires, parents killing their kids, the list goes on and on and on. So when there was a 12 year old boy who was killed by another 12 year old over a FACEBOOK fight. My son no longer wanted to go outside. He could not enjoy the 4th of July because the fireworks sounds like guns. We stayed in a quiet neighborhood but when we visited other people he would cry and not want to get out the car. He would cry, "I want to leave this city and live with my dad."

So I had to make a difficult decision. I had the conversation with their father. He was more than willing to take it on. There was still the issue of the way he was living. I did not like it. It was not like it was unsafe; it was just not stable and different from mine.

Their father and I had countless discussions about trying to make their life with him like life was with me. I wanted the smoothest transition possible for them. Their father was not feeling it. I had to pray and talk to my first lady. Her words were "keep them covered in prayer." That included their father, that he would make the best decisions for "OUR" kids. I had to realize that they were not just my kids. When we were married he was nowhere near the worst dad. Once I put these things in perspective I knew my boys would be ok. This co-parenting thing is not asking permission, but about discussing what our children's needs are and coming up with the best decision for the child.

I bought the boys a phone so I could communicate with my boys. I made plans to see them every month and get them whenever their break was longer than a week. As you can guess in the beginning it was smooth sailing.

After the first couple of months their dad took their phone and was no longer going to help me get them for their fall break. So I had a moment of breakdown and was going to get my boys and never send them back. I went into my savings and got the boys here. To my surprise my nine year old still had fears about being here but wanted to visit. I could not do that to him. I had to realize that right now he being there was for him not me and not their father.

I knew in this moment in time I could not talk to their father, it always turns into yelling, screaming, arguing and getting nothing accomplished. So we communicated through our mutual third party either my husband or his sister. Sometimes communication goes better with others involved.

Through conversing with him I really felt that he in some form still believe I was the person he was married to 9 years ago, and I saw him as the person who divorced me. I just continued to keep everyone involved in my prayers and believe that everything will continue to get better for the sake of "OUR" kids.

FOR OUR KIDS!

Still Learning,

Denna Michelle, A Co-Parent

PS: "This co-parenting thing is not asking permission, but about discussing what our children's needs are and coming up with the best decision for the child." ~DENNA MICHELLE

WHAT IS CO-PARENTING?

Co-parenting describes a parenting situation where the parents are not in a marriage, cohabitation, or romantic relationship with one another. In the United States, "co-parenting" often describes a parenting situation in which two separated or divorced parents take care of their children. Mary McCoy said in her article "What Is Co-Parenting – Definition & Tips for Custody Agreement," The term "co-parenting" was coined to describe a parenting relationship in which the two parents of a child are not romantically involved, but still assume joint responsibility for the upbringing of their child. I gave you two definitions of what Wikipedia says (the site everyone goes to when they don't know something) and a definition from a licensed social worker who works closely with individuals, families, and organizations in crisis. What do you think?

"The term 'co-parent' may also be used to describe a situation where, following divorce or separation, the child's parents seek to maintain equal or equivalent responsibility for the child's upbringing." Can we really have equal responsibility? It's not even equal when two married or cohabitating parents raise a child.

Those definitions make it sound so easy. NOT! According to Wikipedia's definition you're still co-parenting, if for example you are single, but your kids' father does not help; you are still co-parenting. Do you believe that's co-parenting? Then a licensed social worker says that if your kids live in two separate homes at any giving time of the year and the two homes and have disagreements about ways of raising their children you are still co-parenting. Do you believe that's co-parenting? I DON'T!

WHAT CO-PARENT IS NOT?

Co-parenting is not if the parents are separated or divorced and the child lives with their **custodial parent** and go spend some time with their **noncustodial parent**. Here is an example of this situation a child lives with mom on Mondays, Wednesdays every other Thursday, and every other Friday, the other days the child is with their dad. I know you are thinking that is fine they are sharing their child equally. True! That is it they are only sharing days. This is not co-parenting. Another example of this is when the child lives with mom during the school year and goes with dad in summer and on school breaks. Again you are thinking they made an agreement and they are sticking to it. This is not Co-parenting.

Listen to this scenario, mom and dad come to an agreement that the child will stay Mondays, Wednesdays, and every other weekends including Fridays with mom and other days with dad. With the sharing of days the parents also decide that the parent is financially responsible for the child when they have him or her. You say Denna that is definitely Co-parenting. NOPE!

Let's look at some another definitions!

Family therapist Salvador Minuchin emphasizes in his book "Families and Family Therapy" that co-parenting is a supportive partnership between the adults who are responsible for the life of the child. An example of this would be mom and dad come to an agreement that the child will stay Mondays, Wednesdays, and every other weekends including Fridays with mom and other days with dad. With the sharing of days the parents also decide that the parent is financially responsible for the child when they have him or her. The child loves to attend the church his dad is a member of, so the mom to agrees to let the child attend the church every Sunday with dad. Another example would be mom and dad made an agreement that once the child turned 10 that dad would get the child; however the child is going through puberty, so dad decides to let the child stay with mom for 6 more months so the child can adjust to puberty. I hear you saying now if that's not Co-parenting then what is?

 Finally, we got it. The parents made sacrifices to make sure the child was receiving what they needed in life. In one case the child like the religious belief of one parent over the other and because it was important to the child it became important to the mom. In the other case, dad put aside the fact that it was his turn to get his child to have the mom who been through what the child was getting ready to go through begin to guide the child through a new phase in her life. The parents partnered together for the child.

I believe co-parenting is when two parents (together or if they choose not to be together for whatever reason) decides to love their child enough to do what is in the best interest of the child.

So now let's figure out what's in the best interest of your child. "Best interests" are decisions commonly made when parents think about a number of reasons related to the child's situations and the parent situations and abilities to parent, with the child's safety, health, security and well-being as the major concerns. Some examples of these are:

1. How emotionally attached or how close is the relationship between child and parent
2. How safe is the home or environment the child will be in
3. How financially stable the parent is to provide food, clothes and medical
4. How capable is the parent to meet mental and physical needs of the child
5. How mental and physically stable the parent is

These reasons must be considered so that the child cannot and will not be affect by any separation among parents. The child has the right to keep a relationship with both parents, even if they are not together, unless there is an instance of abuse to keep him or her from one or both parents. Keep in mind there are still creative ways a child can keep a relationship with that abusive parent. Letters, supervised visits, phone calls, pictures and even telling positive stories about the absent parent will help the child keep a relationship with that parent.

CO-PARENTING AS PARTNERSHIP

Just like in any business, job, group project or anything where two or more people are working together, it important for all parties to cooperate. My favorite acronym is, T.E.A.M. Together Everyone Achieve More. When mom and dad work together everyone wins. Everyone includes, Grandparents, family members, friends, teachers, daycare workers, church members, the community, and even the WORLD.

So how do we develop a partnership you ask? To partner, each parent needs to become mindful of their own strengths and weaknesses. Knowing your own strengths and weakness helps the other parent to know your needs, your level of understanding, what areas to support, or areas you both need to improve. Areas where both parents need help should lead the parents to find new ways to partner to raise their children, possibly with the help of outside expertise.

Most importantly, to begin partnering, the parents must speak the same language. Language of signals and communications needs to be agreed upon so that when help is needed, the needed help can swing into action. Examples of these could be:

EXAMPLES OF EFFECTIVE PARTNERSHIPS

- Fathers help mothers understand the needs of a growing boy
- Mothers, with a spirit of compassion, try to understand a father's parental insecurities.
- Fathers have—and mothers allow—one-on-one time. Father establishes their own fatherly impulses.
- Both parents understand that, co-parenting, is shared daily acts and routines are valuable opportunities for connection and true shared parental nurturing.
- Mothers don't leave lists of activities for fathers to do with the kids, but allow them to have their own experiences.
- Fathers and mothers don't let child discipline be center of bonding with your child.
- A strong and supportive partnership allows for both parents to have jobs and interests outside the home.
- Sons of co-parenting parents will likely be nurturing fathers themselves.
- Parents don't have to be the same or agree on everything. They can play very different roles as equal partners

- Parents act as supporters. It's OK for one to be overwhelmed, or confused, as the other supports.
- At times, each parent acts as a defense for a child and the other parent.
- Learning as you parent. There is no need to feel perfect. Children will learn from seeing their parents grow as parents.
- Parents can swap roles. There is no need to always be the disciplinarian or nurturer.
- Making enough family time DON'T give up your time with your child to others. Being there is everything!

- "Please step in and take over. I need a break." (Parents acting as a relief)
- "I need your help." (Parents being a support)
- "Let's go talk." (Parents thinking rather than reacting)
- "I would like to handle this." (Parents knowing when not to step in)
- "Please be understanding." (Parents being patient).

The more of these and other signals can be used the more there will be an actual partnership. How these signals work is, you say what is needed and how each parent feels about the way the need can be met. This should be an ongoing mutual conversation. Different parts of the "T.E.A.M." can be focused on at any point without losing site of the whole picture or what holds it together.

An effective co-parenting partnership is one where parents team up to give their child skills where both the parents individual skills combine, support, and better each other for the child's benefit.

CO-PARENTING BENEFITS FOR THE CHILD

One benefits is you have a team that you built from a mom/dad partnership. This is a powerful emotional and behavioral foundation that makes emotionally stable children.

Another benefit is, the child learns to adjust and handle conflict as the parents do in their co-parenting partnership. When co-parenting parents are working together then children reach greater levels of emotional and cognitive development, they are more likely to be calm or be content and do well in school and at home. They would be less likely to get into trouble.

When dads are active from the time their sons are born until they are men, a boys have less chaotic teenage years, and is less aggressive. He knows how to share his feelings. He is able to resolve conflicts. When dads are active in their daughter's life, she has a higher self-esteem, and is less likely to have sex before she wants to, become pregnant, or be a victim of rape.

There are plenty of individual family benefits as well. Which will vary from family to family like mom is less stress, dad more confident, child has more of their needs met, etc. Keep your eyes open when you are co-parenting for your individual family benefits.

CO-PARENTING WHEN YOU DON'T GET ALONG

So you have reached the point where you cannot stand in the same room with your kids' father, what do you do?

The first step is you need to accept the decision you made not be with your child's father. When you don't accept the decision it causes you to suffer emotionally, with other relationships and within your overall life. Accepting the decision simply means you know that at this moment you are not together. The sooner you accept that you are not together the sooner you will be emotional stable, have better relationships and have an overall better life.

The second step is to admit and write down the reasons the relationship did not work. See the relationship from the point of view of the other person. This helps you understand what areas you need to work on to make the partnership of co-parenting work. Don't worry about the other parent. Do it for you child.

The third step is to ask for clarification of things you do not understand. Do this step when both parties are willing and during a calm time. There may need to be a mutual third party or professional to keep everything calm and to stay on task of getting clarification.

The fourth step is anticipate the co-parenting partnership will get better. You can do this step without doing the third step. You should continue to do this step as long as you are co-parenting. Writing downing your expectations and what part you can play to make things better. Pray and be in faith that God will help you through this moment because it is just a moment.

CO-PARENTING TIPS WHEN YOU DON'T GET ALONG

1. Allow your child to keep a relationship with both sides of their family. Ask how the time was to make sure it's a healthy relationship. (Do not compare or compete)
2. Be open to communicate with your children. Allow them to talk and you listen, accept their feelings and make them understand that you will always be there. Choose a positive attitude when talking to your child about the father. (Spare them the details)
3. Communicate with your child's father. You can either use phone, text or evening email. You may need to find a third party who can articulate what you need to say and relay his needs and concerns back to you. (Do not use your child as a go-between)
4. Get your child to believe in you and feel safe. Make your home a safe house where they are respected, taken care of, loved, welcomed, accepted and taught responsibility. It does not matter if you feel the other has little of these what you give will go with your child there.
5. Learn to be resilient. Resiliency is the best gift to give yourself and your child. Show your child and yourself that even when times are hard you survive. You were able to get through that tough time together without falling apart. Develop your child's ability to be optimistic in every area and experience they go through.

DISCIPLINE

DEAR CHILD PUNISHING MOM

I have had my share of moments where I just wanted to... I have had to tell them to walk away. I have had to tell myself to walk away. I have locked myself in the bathroom. If I get upset then I am out of control and out control equals me doing some things I know I will regret as soon as they are done. Sometimes my children's behavior try my patience. Will punishing them really help?

Punishing will help for the moment. Show them what you want them to do and do it when you are calm enough to make the best decision for them and you. This will last a lifetime. "Give a man a fish and you feed him for a day; teach a man to fish and you feed him for a lifetime." Maimonides. Which do you want a day or a lifetime?

I remember growing up and my mom telling me to go to my room until she come in there with my punishment. Waiting for her was worst then any punishment she would give me. Not knowing if I was going to get a whooping, or if I was going to have to stay in my room for a week or the dreaded extra chores.

Chores is another responsibility that I struggle with because it was a punishment growing up I view it as a punishment now. I pay people to clean my house so I don't feel overwhelmed. However, if my mom took the time to guide me in what she ultimately wanted me to do in the first place I would not view cleaning as a punishment but as something that simply needs to be done.

I learn to do my chores that day; however, I did not learn for a lifetime. Discipline should be viewed as correction and guiding your child to live in this world not as a punishment.

Let Guide, Not Punish!

Guiding Our Future,

Denna Michelle, An Educator

PS: "Give a man a fish and you feed him for a day; teach a man to fish and you feed him for a lifetime." ~Maimonides

GUIDE NOT PUNISH

"Chris! I've told you stop messing with Christianna. If you don't stop I am going to knock the wind out of you!" Chris stamped up the stairs. He mumbles under his breath "I hate my life," Mom shouts "Only when you get in trouble. Chris mumbles under his breathe "I hate you!" Mom runs up the stairs…

Unless you are unusual, you have been in a similar situation. Of course, we all know what Chris' mom wanted to teach him: not to tease his sister, and to obey his mother.

Here's what Chris would learn if mom hits him:

- That he has reason to hate people: They will hurt him.

- That he would get hurt by the people closest to him: Who actually love him.

- That it's all right for "big people" to hurt "little people." Which is the reason he picks on his little sister.

- That if a "big" person hurts him, it's a sure sign he has done something wrong: When he gets "big" he will more likely to hurt others when he feels they wronged him.

It is clear that in the hitting Chris' mom didn't teach him what she intended to teach. Instead, she may be teaching hatred, anger, guilt and violence to her son. If mom hits Chris on a regular basis, he may become withdrawn, doubtful, and feel incapable of giving or receiving love. He could become the bully or a juvenile delinquent. He could be pretending to be tough only to hide the hurt he felt. This situation is sad and all too typical. Fortunately, there is a better way to discipline our children.

WHY DISCIPLINE?

There are two purposes to disciplining children. The first: We need to stop certain behaviors. As moms, we have a responsibility to prevent destructive or violent behaviors happening in this world. We cannot allow a toddler to run into the street, a two-year-old to play with grandma's vase, a five-year-old to fall out and have a tantrum, or a teenager to make us buy things that we can't afford. We can stop certain behaviors with rules.

It's important to set these rules wisely.

Without rules we can find ourselves accepting behaviors we really don't want or not enforcing behaviors we do. We go back and forth. Then the child discovers that we don't mean what we say and that they don't need to be obedient.

The second purpose to discipline children has to deal with a lifelong goal that is harder to accomplish. That goal is to teach our children to establish their own limits and rules that come from the beliefs and values after we as moms are not around. We will not be around forever. In other words, moms are responsible for teaching their children self-discipline.

Our children are like a harvest, we need to cultivate the land so that the land is rich to produce the ripened fruit. Prepare the land in that good feeling you have knowing you are doing a good job as a farmer.

Good feelings that develop from discipline are: order, calm, a sense of security and direction. It lets us arrange the parts of our lives into a harmonious lifestyle. It helps us balance our own needs, rights and desires with those of others. What a wonderful skill to teach a child!

With these two goals in mind—keeping behavior within limits and teaching self-discipline—let's go back and look at Chris' Mom again. Did she accomplish the first goal - getting Chris to stop teasing his sister? For now Chris might leave his sister alone, but only for a while. He may not tease his sister while mom is around, but what happens when she is not around.

What about her long term goals? Teaching him to love his sister, to care about her feelings and safety and to respect her rights? Instead, the slap on his behind may have taught him resentment, hatred, fear, and avoidance.

Disciplining a child often turns out to be a confusing and emotional experience.

That's why it is helpful to keep the two goals of discipline firmly in mind. They can help you tell the difference between your need to guide your child's behavior, and your need to release stress.

RESPONIBLE

DEAR IRRESPONSIBLE MOM

There was a time in my life where I was an irresponsible mom. We all have that moment. Either from guilt of always doing things for your kids or from not having a childhood or just the weight of the world on our shoulders.

My issue was I had just gotten divorced and was mad at the world. The world owed me and my kids a man who loved, respected and provided for us. Apparently the world didn't know that and because it didn't I got depressed. I would stay in the bed all day. I would not eat and was barely sleeping. I only got up to go to the bathroom. I wasn't too depressed to go to the bathroom on myself. HAHAHA!

Responsibility Tips:

1. Do what you say you're going to do
2. Persevere: keep on trying
3. Make your best effort
4. Use self-control
5. Be self-disciplined
6. Think before you act
7. Consider the consequences
8. Be accountable for your choice

My kids who were 4, 3, and 1 at the time had to fend for themselves. I was worried about what I did and how to make it better. My sister would come and try to make me feel better. All could think was I have no husband, no money, and no house, so I thought.

I went to church and received a revelation. That if I did it before I can do it again. I must learn from my mistakes and not let anything take me out my character. My character was protecting my children part of the reason I was no longer married. I got a three bedroom place to stay. I got a great job as a head start teacher, started my own family daycare and started a program that helped low income moms to become self-sufficient. I got remarried to my AWESOME husband I have now. I did this to make sure my kids had everything they needed. I accomplished all this because I took the big step in taking responsibility for my mistakes and learned from them.

Let's Step Up!

Stepping Up,

Denna Michelle, Responsible Person

PS: "PS: "The one thing that all imperfectly perfect moms have is the gift to become responsible. ~ Denna Michelle

CHARACTER OF RESPONSIBLE MOM

Responsible moms are good moms who have true character. Having true character is the way you really are when no one is looking. Good moms don't do good things for show or credit but as a face of their true selves. Good moms are moms of action! They take care of themselves and their families. They can be depended on to do the right thing even when the right thing is hard to do. Responsible moms help their children, neighbors, kids' teachers and friends, make an effort and do their best.

The responsible mom does her greatest on any task. The responsible mom completes the whole job, not just part of it. So when your teen is hanging out with the wrong crowd don't give up on him or her keep trying to reach them. Even when it gets worse, your determination to help your teen can not fade. Once you started, you must be responsible enough to finish it (even if you don't want to)! Get help if you must.

What RESPONSIBILITY Looks like!

1. Responsibility is accepting the results of your own actions. If you have acted unkindly to someone it is your responsibility to apologize. If you have chosen to tell a lie you must be responsible enough to understand why others may not trust you.
2. You are not only responsible for yourself, but also for your family. You cannot control the actions of your kids; however, from the beginning you can guide them to choose to do what's right. You can guide your kids to complete their responsibilities for example, their school work, their chores, cleanliness and taking care of their own bodies, etc.

3. Decide that your actions will be positive, then your kids will choose positive ones. Only share positive or encouraging statements with kids. Act in a way that lifts up both your kids and yourself. Let your face give off kindness and a positive attitude (smile a lot)! Be patient and have fun.
4. The responsible mom is sensitive to the feelings of her kids! The responsible mom understands that her children who are physically challenged need friends and encouragement, not a whooping. The responsible mom recognizes when her kids feel alone, and offers them a helping hand and emotional support. The responsible mom knows when her kids are having a hard day and can offer a listening ear. Remember to be their mom not their friend. Know when to push and when not to. Gain discernment to know when.
5. Be responsible by staying away from alcohol & drugs. Alcohol & Drugs can ruin your reputation (good character). Alcohol & Drugs can alter or change the way you think and act. Be responsible by staying away from those who have or do drugs.
6. Be responsible with your money: Save for an emergency. Think before you spend – "Do I really need this?" Have one specific place to keep your money (never leave it in your pockets or lying around). Don't be tight with your money PLAN how you will spend it. Toss the guilt! Some of us moms spend all our money on bills and our children TOSS THE GUILT! Plan to spend some on you every once in a while. Others of us spend it all on ourselves. TOSS THE GUILT! Plan to do fun things with your

child. Lastly we spend it all on bills, TOSS THE GUILT! Plan and balance. Spend on yourself and your child.

"The price of greatness is responsibility." - Sir Winston Churchill

RESPONSIBILITIES TO YOUR CHILD

You are responsible for:

1. Making tough decision for them and showing them the process.
2. Holding them accountable for things they say.
3. Teaching when to be dependent and independent.
4. Teaching them to do their best and to know it's ok to make mistakes as long as they learn from them.

You are NOT responsible for:

1. Their happiness
2. Control of what choices they make
3. What their ability to do and not do
4. Making them perfect

QUOTES

Enough! It's time to grow up. If we want to play adult games—living our Dream—we must play by adult rules. One of the primary adult rules: We are individually responsible for our own lives." ~John Roger and Peter McWilliam

"Ninety-nine percent of all failures come from people who have a habit of making excuses." ~George Washington Carver

Motherhood is always a sweet responsibility never an opportunity

You are responsible for the gift that has been entrusted you. YOUR CHILD, so GO RAISE THEM! ~unknown

Quotes have been taken from www.brainyquotes.com

PERSEVERE

DEAR HOPELESS MOM,

As a woman who was divorced with three children, I had so many hats on. The hats were keeping me tired, frustrated, sad and angry. I saw the same characteristics in my kids and I decided it was time for a change. I got a REVELATION or vision that although I was wearing so many hats I was making the least impact on the most important HAT, being a mom. I was not there for my children the way I wanted to be. I knew something had to change not only for me but for my family.

Being separated from my first husband since 2008 and not getting remarried until 2013, there were very hard times. I was with my first husband for 4 years which he helped me with the kids. I did little to no discipline, cooking or cleaning. To having to do it all until I remarried.

When we separated the kids were 3, 2 and 9 months. Let me give you a picture of this. One kid coming out but not fully out his "Terrible Twos" and one in his "Terrible Twos. Then there is the 9 month old who has now began to walk and is "Exploring" the world. There was never a moment of rest.

My ex-husband lived in Atlanta, GA and I lived in Milwaukee, WI. He rarely saw them and would send money every blue moon. Regular contact had never been maintained and contact was on an ad hoc or unplanned basis. I know you're asking what support I really had as a single parent.

My family, friends and church family were always willing to help. But going from a 5 bedroom 3 bath house to sharing a 2 bedroom with my mom was a wakeup call for me. I found it difficult to ask family or friends for help. I let my pride get in the way.

My pride had me go through some ups and some downs. It was very trying time financially. I had just graduated from college, and I didn't have a job. I had to get state assistance for medical, childcare and food. Not knowing when the dad would send any money.

So eight months later, I decided to do something I swore I would never do. TEACH. I applied to be a head start teacher and got the position teaching three year olds and then coming home to my own 2, 4 and 5 year old. Crazy right!

My kids were acting up in school. One hitting teachers, and other kids with chairs. One kid was found touching girls in the bathroom, and the last one cried every day I dropped her off to school. I had to get help. I was going to work taking great care of all the three year olds that came into my classroom for three years. I would either come home and ignore mine or focus on punishment. I called in my mom, sisters, brothers and my church family. They rallied together and they became the village it took to raise my kids.

I thought I could never be a good single parent. I had 2 real weaknesses; I didn't cook or clean. I had to get help for the areas I lacked in. I even had my Mother in law come and live with me to help me while I work, and to have a mental break when I came home. Then when she told me she was moving I opened up my own family childcare so I didn't have to pay for childcare. I never really was alone, I always had help.

But I then realized I could do this thing called be a SINGLE MOM.

We moved into our own three bedroom, I was doing good on my job for three years, paid off my car, gave it away, bought a truck, started a daycare, and the kids behaviors begin to be manageable. I woke up three years later and realized I created a home for my family by MYSELF, with support of my family, friends and church family. It became more obvious that we were much better off and more stable on our own.

So many people learn for hindsight, learn to learn what your weaknesses are and let someone who is strong in those areas help you. You have to continue to keep going no matter how hopeless your situation looks. You must persevere to bring revelation to your situation.

GET VISION TO PERSEVERE!!

Sincerely,

Denna M. Triggs, Visionary

PS: WHERE THERE IS NO REVELATION, PEOPLE CAST OFF RESTRAINT; BUT BLESSED IS THE ONE WHO HEEDS WISDOM'S INSTRUCTION.   ~ PROVERBS 29:18NEW INTERNATIONAL VERSION (NIV)

WHY MOMS DON'T PERSEVERE: EXCUSES

You could have made every excuse in the book, don't. Making excuses will eliminate your opportunity to grow. Excuses will cause you to stay where you are irresponsible and lost. I was at a point in my life where I had to choose to persevere or make excuses.

Merriam-Webster dictionary says, "an excuse is to try to remove blame from". Excuses are reasons we make to ourselves about things, people, actions and situations. Excuses are made up reasons to stay the same. We make reasons for our behavior, to not do something, or simply as not taking responsibility. Excuses are a source of putting the responsibility or blame of a problem on your conditions.

WHY MOMS DON'T PERSEVERE: FEAR

Fear tricks us to stay in our comfort zone. Fear grows as a result of not understanding, not enough information or resources, and a lack of experience or perspective. If you lack all these things, you will naturally lack confidence, and as a result you will be unsuccessful at achieving your goals and tasks. So you will tend to get comfortable with your life and circumstances in order to increase your confidence.

Nevertheless, all you're really achieving is a false sense of confidence. The pain is still there, and the pain will continue until persevere, and finally overcome your fears.

Fears you need to overcome:

Fear of Failure	Fear of Uncertainty
Fear of Embarrassment	Fear of Responsibility
Fear of Success	Fear of Making Mistakes
Fear of Change	

HOW TO PERSEVERE

To persevere we must first look at overcoming all of your excuses and fears. Perseverance is something that every mom possess. The difficult thing is that most mothers hold on to their excuses and fears, because it is easier than changing. Here is some tips for persevering:

1. *Have awareness*. **Before you can persevere, you must know that fear and excuses create confusion in your life. It is easy to get attached to fears and excuses that you think are your reality, which couldn't be further from the truth. It is just as easy to persevere as it is to think about your fears and excuses.**

Know exactly what you're afraid of. Look at what is happening around you when you are in a state of fear. What is happening to my body? What am I really scared of? If you don't have a good memory, write it down.

Things to write down:

1. What am I settling for?
2. What fears do I have?
3. Why am I fearful?
4. How do these fears prevent me from moving forward?
5. How do these fears hinder my ability to get what I want?

You need to be aware of what you are afraid so you can speak the positive and visualize what you want.

2. *Get some vision:* **Seeing what you want is a part of vision. Vision is, to have a clear understanding of where you want to go. Thoughts are the first step toward manifestation, and the clearer they are, the more quickly and easily you can make them real.**

a. Hold an image of yourself having reached your goal successfully. See yourself standing beside your well behaved child (perhaps in new surroundings). You might include a picture of your family smiling as the centerpiece.
b. Hold onto your vision. As you work toward your goals things will happen or not happen that will make it seem like you will never reach your goal. It may take some time, but it will happen through perseverance.

3. *Structure an action plan:* **Create** actual steps you can take toward your goal. Include both short-term and long-term plans.
    a. Create a schedule. Practice discipline by sticking to that schedule, even when you don't feel like it. (This leaves less time for unwanted behaviors)
    b. Take baby steps. Trying to change them all at once will be overwhelming for you and your child. Take things one step at a time. Breaking it down makes it feel more doable.
    c. Create options. Have one or more backup plans. Your backup plan may include ways to support yourself when you get stressed out or outside help to support the family as whole
    d. Keep your spirits up. Hope and expectation are powerful forces that can brings success to you and your family. Give yourself and your child rewards as you accomplish each step of your action plan, and give yourself breaks to renew your mind when the going gets really tough.
4. *Practice patience.* Be realistic about how long it will take to achieve your vision of discipline. Remember motherhood

does not always provide a clear path toward your goal of being a perfect mom. Children do not come with manuals. You may run into obstacles and emotional blocks along the way, so be prepared to tackle them.

5. *Get support.* It takes a village, surround yourself with people, especially other moms, who believe in and encourage you. Have someone who is willing to listen to you when you feel frustrated and not judge you or make you feel worse.

   a. Don't believe everything you hear. There are people who will try to discourage and we as moms tend to believe that if someone tells us something it must be true. What is really important is your own truth and your belief in yourself as a perfect mom, and holding onto that for dear life.

   b. *Professional Help:* **Professional help gives you access to skills and resources that you don't already have. Help like this can give you someone you can be accountable to, who will not let you off the hook because something didn't work out and you got discouraged.**

   c. Spend time with moms who share your passion. Explore new ways of motherhood through classes and experiences of other moms.

Your process is different from the next person. But there is a process.

CLOSING

DEAR IMPERFECTLY PERFECT MOM,

Remember there is no such thing as a perfect mom; however, you can be imperfectly perfect. Use this book to develop your knowledge, habits and confidence you need to be a successful mom! Remember it is ok to be imperfect and that is what makes you perfect.

GAIN WISDOM!

WISDOM IS APPLIED KNOWLEDGE.

IF YOU KNOW BETTER THAN YOU SHOULD DO BETTER.

INSANITY IS REPEATING THE SAME THING OVER AND OVER

Gaining Wisdom,

Denna Michelle, IMPERFECTLY PERFECT MOM

PS: NOW WHATEVER PRINCIPLE YOU WANT TO USE, USE IT! IF YOU START SMALL AND SEE IT THROUGH YOU WILL STILL SEE BIG RESULTS.

RESOURCES

DEAR IMPERFECTLY PERFECT MOM:

Quotes have been taken from www.brainyquotes.com

Salvador Minuchin, "Families and Family Therapy" Jan 31, 1974

https://www2.highlights.com/newsroom/national-survey-reveals-62-kids-think-parents-are-too-distracted-listen

http://2012books.lardbucket.org/pdfs/a-primer-on-communication-studies.pdf

Denna Michelle, IMPERFECTLY PERFECT MOM

ABOUT THE AUTHOR

DENNA M TRIGGS

Denna Michelle Triggs is a self-motivated mother, wife, and entrepreneur. That's just a few of the great things about her that shines. Denna is a beautiful strong independent woman who knows how to take care of business.

As an author Denna gets her inspiration from her pastors of many years Dr. Anthony D Burns and Robin L Burns. With the love of God, Denna spends most of her time at church as a Director. Helping ministries grow and providing leadership. Denna gain acceptance to sharing her vision of being successful.

Denna has her Bachelor's Degree in Community Education. Denna has worked in school and daycare settings. Also with owning her own businesses she shares the wealth of knowledge by helping and coaching others and inspires them to see their vision and fulfill their dreams.

Denna enjoys spending time with her family. She has 5 wonderful children 4 boys and 1 girl. As a wonderful wife, a caring mother, a loving daughter, a great sister and friend, Denna cares deeply for those around her and wants the best for them. And now she wants the best for you.

As she progresses in life and continues her journey of success her books will be an inspiration to all those who sets their eyes on them. Denna looks forward to introducing herself and wishes you blessed and beloved life.

SUGGESTED READINGS:

DEAR IMPERFECTLY PERFECT MOM:

Here are a list of great books that have helped me to become a PROUD IMPERFECTLY PERFECT MOM:

The Seven Habits of Highly Effective Families, by Stephan R. Covey

Positive Discipline, by Jane Nelson

Reinventing Yourself: When the Brook Dries Up, by Dr. Anthony D. Burns

It's All About the Children, by Robin L. Burns

The Power of a Made Up Mind: The Battle Within, by Min. Sharon D. Brumfield

You Better Believe God, by Minister Nina Haliburton

Strength to Endure, by Sharan P. Fifer

Re-Focus, Re-Imagine, Re-Charge: 21 Days of Choosing You, by Dr. Melissa J. Bonds

Financial Peace University, by Dave Ramsey

www.ingramcontent.com/pod-product-compliance
Lightning Source LLC
Chambersburg PA
CBHW070101100426
42743CB00012B/2622